754020787

OREM HIGH SCHOOL MEDIA CENTER
OREM, UTAH 84058

CALL NO. 616.95 DATE 1993
McC

Sexually Transmitted Diseases

by Mark McCauslin

CRESTWOOD HOUSE

New York
Maxwell Macmillan Canada
Toronto
Maxwell Macmillan International
New York   Oxford   Singapore   Sydney

LIBRARY OF CONGRESS CATALOGING-IN-PUBLICATION DATA

McCauslin, Mark.
   Sexually transmitted diseases / by Mark McCauslin. — 1st ed.
     p.   cm. — (Facts about)
   Includes glossary/index.
   Summary: Discusses sexually transmitted diseases, what they are, how they are spread, and how they can be treated.
   ISBN 0-89686-720-X
   1. Sexually transmitted diseases—Juvenile literature. [1. Sexually transmitted diseases.] I. Title. II. Series: Facts About
RC200.M393   1992
616.95'1—dc20   91-18445

PHOTO CREDITS
Cover: Jeff Greenberg
Jeff Greenberg: 4, 6-7, 10, 13, 19, 21, 23, 27, 30, 33, 36, 39, 43
Ned Matura: 16
Alison Blake: 41

Copyright ©1992 by CRESTWOOD HOUSE, Macmillan Publishing Company

All rights reserved. No part of this book may be reproduced or transmitted in any form or by any means, electronic or mechanical, including photocopying, recording, or by any information storage and retrieval system, without permission in writing from the Publisher.

Crestwood House
Macmillan Publishing Company
866 Third Avenue
New York, NY 10022

Maxwell Macmillan Canada, In
1200 Eglinton Avenue East
Suite 200
Don Mills, Ontario M3C 3N1

Macmillan Publishing Company is part of the Maxwell Communication Group of Companies.

First edition

Printed in the United States of America

10 9 8 7 6 5 4 3 2 1

CONTENTS

Joey's Secret	4
What Are Sexually Transmitted Diseases?	8
Kim's Story: Gonorrhea	10
Frank's Story: Syphilis	14
Marissa's Story: Herpes	18
Gene's Story: AIDS	21
Other STDs	28
Vaginitis	28
Chlamydia infections	29
Genital warts	29
Scabies and lice	31
Maybe It Will Go Away	32
What Should I Do?	35
Treatments and Cures	37
Telling Partners	38
Next Time: Prevention	41
Feeling Good about Yourself	43
For More Information	45
Glossary/Index	46–48

STD stands for sexually transmitted disease, a disease that one person can pass on to another while having sexual relations.

JOEY'S SECRET

Joey opens the door to the health center and nervously glances around the waiting room. His gaze rests on the rack of pamphlets in the corner. As he heads toward it, he hopes no one is watching him.

The colorful pamphlets seem to swirl in front of his eyes. Suddenly he feels sick to his stomach. He wonders if it is because he is nervous, or if the nausea is another *symptom* of whatever ailment he has.

Yesterday he noticed a small, irritated sore on his penis. The sore isn't very big or painful. But Joey is afraid it's a symptom of some kind of *venereal disease.*

He thinks back to the party he went to two weeks ago. He'd ended up in bed with a girl he had just met. Joey had regretted the encounter the next morning. Now he is angry and embarrassed. He'd been stupid to have sex with a stranger without using a *condom.*

Joey grabs a few pamphlets on *sexually transmitted diseases.* He stuffs them into his jacket pocket and leaves the health center. When he gets back to his dorm room, he locks the door and spreads out the pamphlets before him.

Reading the pamphlets only makes him feel worse. He is now convinced that he does have a sexually transmitted disease. But he is not sure what disease he has. According to the booklets, the sore he has could be a symptom of a number of diseases. He worries that it could even be a symptom of AIDS.

The last thought scares Joey so much that his hands begin to tremble. He thinks, Why me? Why did this have to happen to me? He throws himself on his bed, not sure what to do next.

Nobody wants to get a sexually transmitted disease, so everyone needs to know how to protect himself or herself against them. It is important to take precautions to keep from getting infected. It is also very important to recognize the symptoms of sexually transmitted diseases as well as to know how to take care of yourself

During the 1960s, increased sexual freedom in our society introduced a wider variety of diseases.

if you do get one. This book will help you find the answers.

WHAT ARE SEXUALLY TRANSMITTED DISEASES?

There are many different types of diseases that one person can pass on to another through having sexual relations. Some of these diseases have existed for thousands of years. Others began to spread when Christopher Columbus and other explorers first sailed the globe. The sailors on these ships were exposed to new germs, and diseases such as syphilis soon spread through the population. Other diseases, like herpes and AIDS, have only recently become widespread problems.

At one time, the term venereal disease (VD) referred to two common diseases: *syphilis* and *gonorrhea*. During the 1960s, however, increased sexual freedom in our society led to the spread of a wider variety of diseases.

Syphilis and gonorrhea still exist. But *herpes, AIDS, genital warts, lice* and *scabies* are now widespread as well.

All of these diseases are now referred to by doctors as sexually transmitted diseases (STDs). They are caused by *bacteria, viruses* or *parasites* that are transmitted during intimate body contact.

Bacteria are extremely tiny plants that live in men, women, and animals, as well as in plants, soil, and water. Because they are so small, they cannot be seen by the human eye. Not all bacteria are harmful to us. But some bacteria cause diseases such as syphilis and gonorrhea.

Viruses are germs like bacteria, but they are even smaller. They exist only in people, animals and plants. Viruses cause many different problems in people. Short-term ailments, such as the flu or warts, are caused by viruses. And viruses cause several kinds of STDs, including AIDS and herpes.

Parasites are organisms that live on other organisms, called *hosts*. Parasites get the nutrients they need from the hosts' blood. Fleas and leeches are examples of parasites, as are scabies and lice. Because scabies and lice are very often passed from one person to another during intimate contact, they are considered to be STDs.

Most STDs have cures, but some do not. STDs that are caused by bacteria or parasites can usually be cured through the use of certain medications. There are fewer medications that kill viruses.

KIM'S STORY: GONORRHEA

Kim sat in the doctor's waiting room, flipping the pages of a magazine. Every time the door to the examination room opened, she looked up expectantly. She was waiting for her doctor to tell her the results of her tests.

Most STDs can be treated with antibiotics, which a doctor can prescribe.

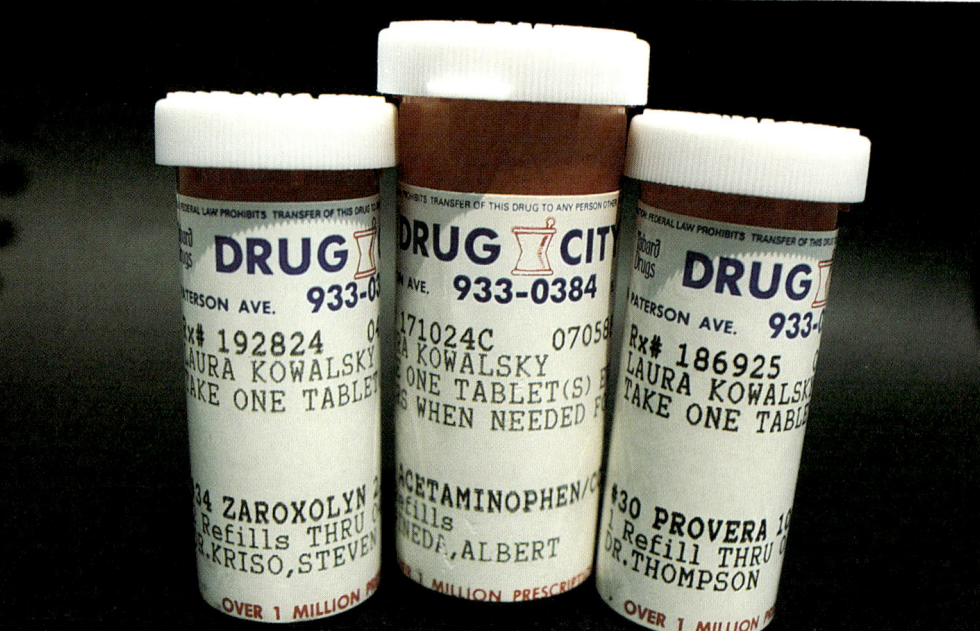

She kept saying to herself that the tests were just routine, that she was fine. She was experiencing a little pain in her lower stomach, but she didn't think it was a big deal. She was sorry she had even mentioned it to the doctor last week during her checkup. But since she had started taking the Pill, she knew it was important to report anything out of the ordinary to her doctor. He had warned her that she might experience some side effects from the birth control pills. Now it looked as if she was.

The door opened again. This time the doctor appeared and motioned for her to come in. He got right to the point.

"Kim, I have some distressing news for you. It's nothing to panic about, because there is a cure. But you have gonorrhea."

"What? There must be some mistake." But even as she said the words, her cheeks flushed red in embarrassment.

"I'm afraid not," the doctor said. "I know that you are on the Pill, but you haven't been practicing safer sex, have you?"

"No," she answered. When he had prescribed the birth control pills to her, he had explained that the pills would protect her from unwanted pregnancy—but not from sexually transmitted diseases. He'd told her that a good way to protect herself from STDs was to make sure that her partners used condoms. This is called practicing *safer sex*.

Kim's story is a familiar one to many doctors. Every

year, more than two million people develop gonorrhea. Most patients with gonorrhea are between the ages of 20 and 30.

Two to six days after sexual intercourse with an infected person, the symptoms of gonorrhea may begin to appear. In men, the main symptoms are a burning feeling while urinating or a yellowish discharge from the penis which looks like pus. Women may have a cloudy discharge or abnormal bleeding from the vagina, or some discomfort in their abdomens.

Frequently there are no symptoms at all. This is dangerous because the person with gonorrhea can spread the disease to someone else without knowing it. That is why there are so many cases every year.

People can also develop gonorrhea in the mouth or anus. Often infection in these sites causes very minor symptoms or no symptoms at all.

A doctor can cure gonorrhea with *penicillin* or other *antibiotics*. If untreated, gonorrhea can spread to other parts of the body and do damage there. Women run the risk of not being able to have children if they don't treat the disease as soon as they notice the warning signs.

Women run the risk of not being able to have children if they don't receive treatment as soon as they notice the warning signs of gonorrhea.

FRANK'S STORY: SYPHILIS

Frank yawned and threw the covers off himself. He got out of bed and opened the curtains. The bright morning sun shone down on him as he nervously slipped out of his pajamas.

He breathed a sigh of relief. The sore was now gone. He had thought it might be a symptom of a sexually transmitted disease, but now he knew it couldn't have been. If it had been a disease, the sore would not have gone away. Or, at least he thought so.

Frank walked over to his desk and picked up a piece of paper that his friend Pete had given him. A phone number and a doctor's name were on the paper. When Frank had confided in Pete about the sore, Pete had suggested he call his doctor.

Frank grabbed the phone and dialed Pete.

"Good news," Frank said when his friend picked up. "I was mistaken. The sore went away, so I don't have to call your doctor."

"Are you sure?" Pete asked. "Just because the sore went away doesn't mean you don't have a disease. That's what I've always heard, anyway. Why don't you make an appointment with the doctor? He'll be able to tell you one way or the other."

Frank sighed, annoyed. Pete was his best friend, but

he had a habit of butting his nose into Frank's personal life. He was always giving Frank unwanted advice.

For example, last month he and Pete had gone to their favorite bar and met a girl named Sheila. They had seen her there before. Frank knew she had a reputation for sleeping with a lot of different guys.

When Sheila started to flirt with Frank, he had told Pete he would see him later. He was going to introduce himself to her and, he hoped, ask her to go home with him.

Frank thought that any other friend would have said "Go for it" or "Good luck." But what had Pete done? He'd given Frank a lecture on safer sex. Pete could be a real drag sometimes, Frank thought. Frank had ignored his advice that night, and he was planning to ignore his advice now.

"Look, Pete," Frank said into the receiver. "If I had some sort of disease, I'd be sick, right? But I'm not. And I don't even have the sore anymore. I wouldn't even know what to say to the doctor."

"You could say that you had unsafe sex with someone. You could ask to have some tests done to see if you have a sexually transmitted disease."

Frank had had enough of Pete's lecturing. "Why don't you mind your own business!" he yelled into the phone, then slammed the receiver down. In anger, Frank tore up the scrap of paper with the doctor's name.

I don't need the doctor, or Pete's friendship either, Frank said to himself. I can take care of myself.

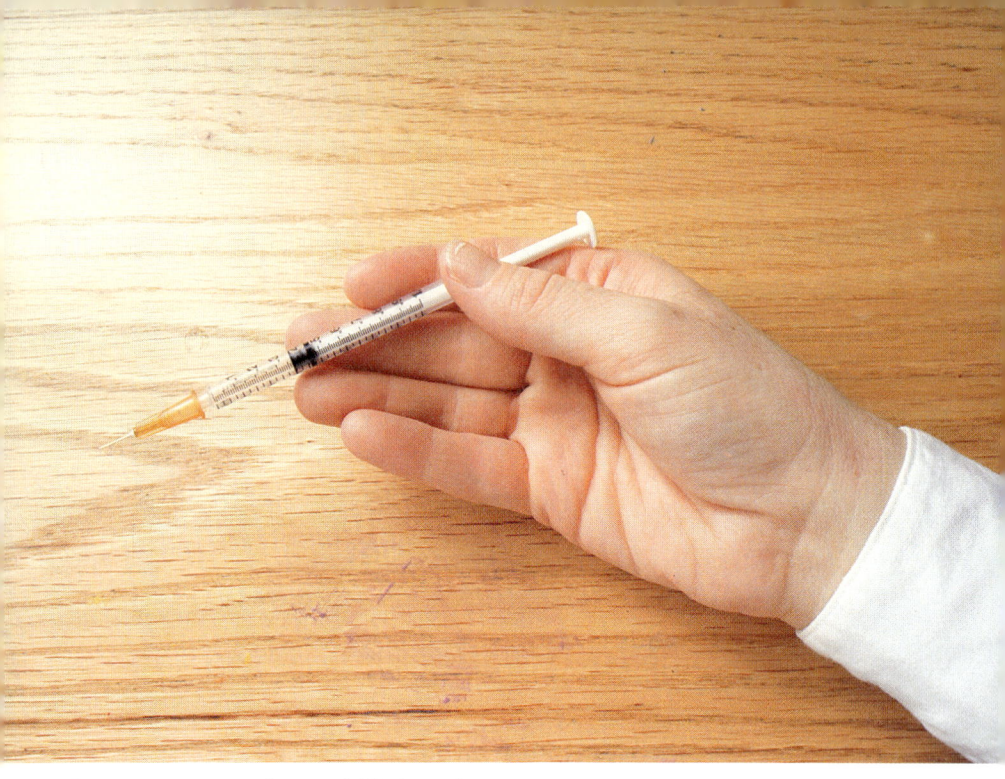

A common cure for syphilis is a shot of penicillin.

Three weeks passed before Frank spoke to Pete again. And when he called Pete, his tone was apologetic.

"I'm sorry I was such a jerk," he said into the phone.

"Are you okay, Frank?" Pete asked. He sounded concerned when he heard the tone in Frank's voice.

"I, er, think I have the flu. I have all the symptoms, but I have a rash, too." Frank paused and then went on. "Actually, I'm calling to say I'm sorry *and* to ask you for that doctor's name and number. I think you might be right. I think I have an STD."

Frank's story is not uncommon with people who have

syphilis, as he does. The first symptom of syphilis is a *chancre* (pronounced "shanker"). A chancre is a hard, painless, red sore. About two or three weeks after a person is infected, a chancre will appear on the sex organs, breasts, lips, fingers, or in the rectum or mouth.

Because chancres are painless, a person with the disease may not be aware of the sore, especially if it appears inside the sex organs, rectum or mouth. The chancre usually disappears after two or three weeks. Because some people don't feel or see the sore, and because the sore goes away, many people don't go to the doctor at this time.

The next stage of the disease is called *secondary syphilis*. It occurs two to six weeks after the chancre heals. The most common symptom is a skin rash that often appears on the palms or on the soles of the feet. Symptoms may also include fever, headaches, loss of appetite and weariness.

If an infected person does not go to the doctor during secondary syphilis, the next stage he or she will develop is called *latent syphilis*. This stage can lead to major problems. A person with latent syphilis can become paralyzed, insane or blind.

Luckily, the syphilis bacteria can be killed by shots of penicillin or other antibiotics. It is easier to spread the disease during the first and secondary stages. It is also easier for a patient to be treated effectively during these stages. Therefore, it is important for an infected person to seek treatment as soon as possible.

MARISSA'S STORY: HERPES

"What's wrong, Alice?" Marissa asked her friend, who seemed upset. "Did you and James have a fight?"

"No, but I think I'm going to break up with him. He just told me he has herpes! I can't date someone with herpes. I need to think about my future, and marrying someone with herpes is out of the question."

"But you like James so much. Can't you try to be a little more understanding?"

"That's easy for you to say, Marissa. You and Alan have each other. You don't need to worry about this sort of thing."

Marissa shook her head. "Our marriage is great, but it's not as perfect as you might think, Alice. In fact, Alan has herpes, too."

"Really? Did you know this before you married him?" Alice asked.

"Alan told me about it before we ever slept together, but I didn't stop caring about him. We've learned to live with it."

"But aren't you afraid of catching herpes?"

"Of course," Marissa said, "but Alan and I take precautions. He knows when he is about to get an outbreak. When he gets these warning signs, we don't

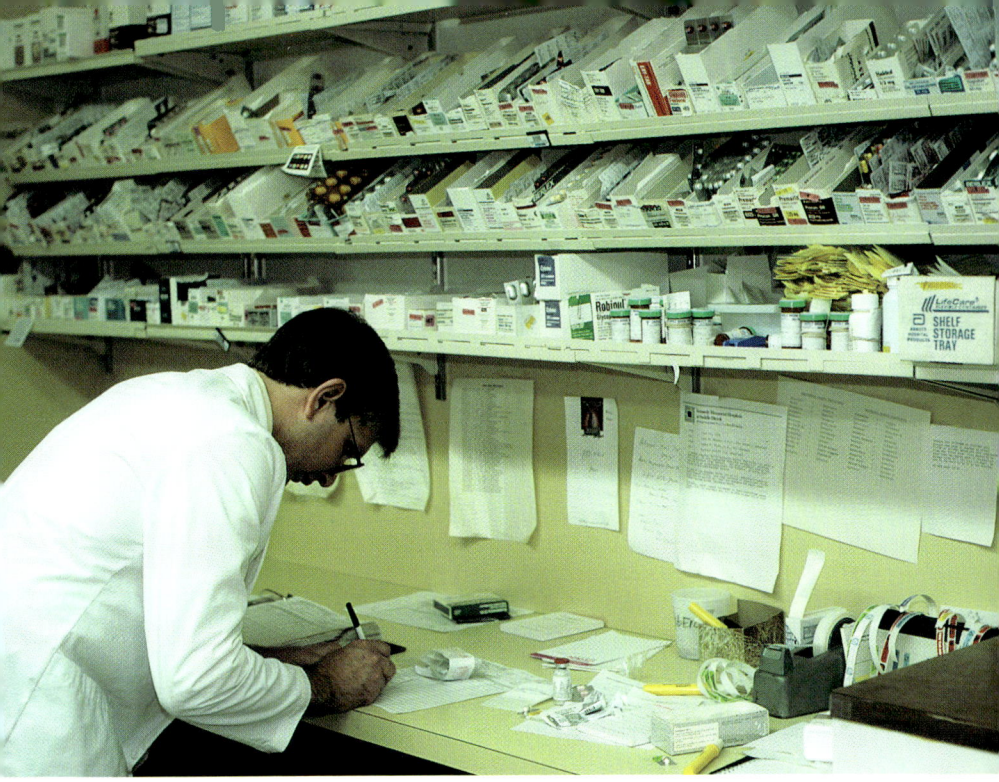

Physicians run tests to determine if a patient has an STD.

have physical contact. And as added protection, we always use condoms when we make love."

"But don't you want to have kids someday? How can you if you always have safer sex?"

"We just have to be careful that Alan is completely healed when we try. It's not like he always is broken out, you know. In fact, as time passes, his outbreaks become more and more infrequent. And each outbreak is less severe, so the sores clear up faster."

"You make your situation sound so easy," Alice said in admiration.

"Well, I wouldn't say it's easy," Marissa responded,

"but when you're in love with someone, you can overcome almost any obstacle."

In the United States, about 20 million people are infected with the herpes virus. And 500 thousand new cases are reported every year. Genital herpes is spread by direct physical contact, usually by sexual intercourse.

About six days after being exposed to the virus, an infected person will probably feel a tingling or burning sensation on his or her sex organs or mouth. Within hours, blisters will develop on the infected area. The person may also have a fever, headache or muscle ache.

During the next two to three weeks the blisters will dry up and go away. Unfortunately, the virus never goes away. It moves to the person's spine. It may stay there for a few days, or it may be there for a number of years. Under certain conditions, the virus may be triggered. The virus will return to the sex organs or the mouth, and the process of infection will start again. This is called a *recurrence.*

Stress, illness, too much sun, menstruation and even sex are all things that can bring on a recurrence. As time passes, recurrences generally become less severe. There is also more time between each recurrence.

Some people feel a burning or tingling sensation just before a recurrence. Other people do not experience the warning signs. Because the virus can be spread a few days before sores actually appear, people with herpes should always use condoms. This is the best way to prevent the spread of the virus.

Although there is no cure for herpes, there are several medications that a doctor can prescribe. These help heal the herpes blisters as well as help prevent recurrences.

GENE'S STORY: AIDS

As the lights went on in the theater, Gene and his brother, Ed, rose from their seats and walked out. Ed asked Gene if he wanted to go out for coffee.

"No, thanks," Gene answered. "I'm really tired."

Coming to terms with AIDS can be difficult. But more and more people are learning to lead active lives with this disease.

Ed was immediately concerned. "Are you okay?"

Gene nodded to reassure his brother. "Why shouldn't I be tired? I was at the office in the morning. Then I worked out at the gym. And that movie was more than two hours long."

Ed was still concerned. Gene had been in the hospital four weeks before because he had had pneumonia. That was when Ed had learned that his brother was sick with AIDS.

"Look, Ed," Gene said, "I've given up drinking and junk food. I get plenty of sleep and exercise. I've been taking my medicine. I'm going to beat this thing, so stop worrying about me."

Ed couldn't help being worried about his brother. He knew that several of Gene's friends had died of AIDS. They had taken care of themselves, too, but in the end that hadn't seemed to matter.

Yet Gene did appear to be very healthy. And a few of Gene's friends with AIDS were still going strong, although they had been infected for a number of years.

The brothers said good-bye when they reached Gene's apartment building. Ed watched as Gene walked up the stairs. Suddenly Gene grasped the railing and turned very pale. Ed ran up the stairs to help him. He opened the apartment door and led Gene to the couch.

"I guess I'm more tired than I thought," Gene said weakly. "Maybe I did too much today."

Ed decided to spend the night on the couch. He wanted to be sure Gene was going to be okay. When Ed

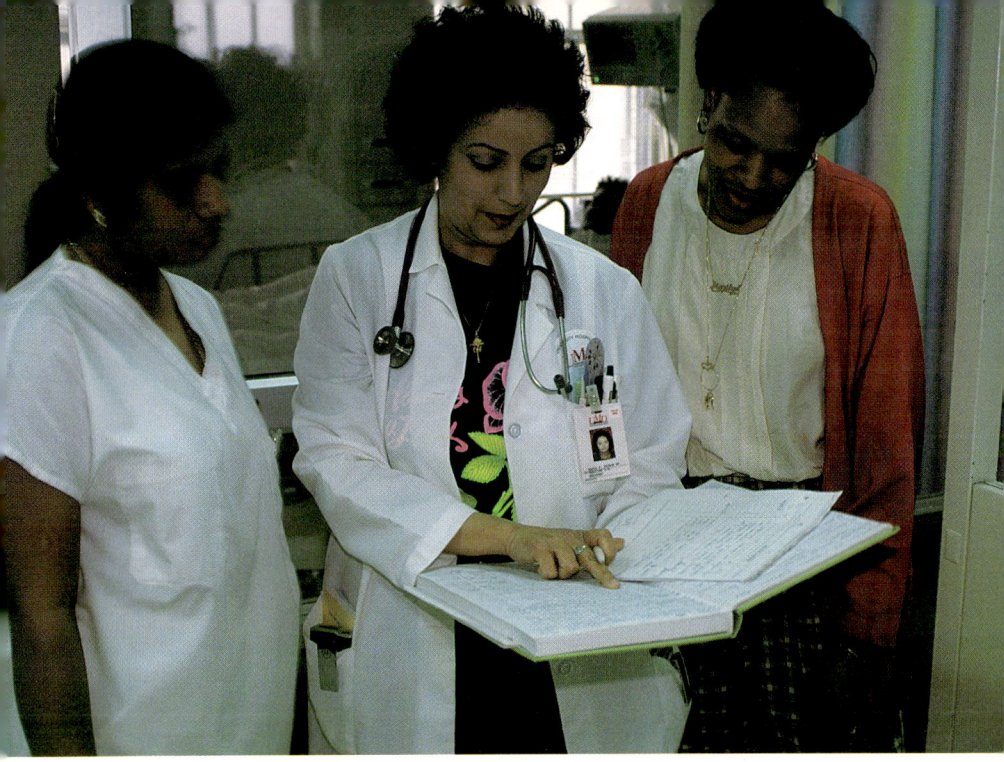

Doctors and researchers are still working on a cure for AIDS.

helped Gene get ready for bed, he noticed that his brother was very skinny. He also had several dark spots on his chest and arm. Now Gene didn't seem to be as healthy as Ed thought.

The next morning Gene was still tired, but otherwise he was back to normal. It was as if nothing had happened. Ed wondered how a person with AIDS could be so sick one day and then seem to be better the next. He realized he had a lot more to learn about this strange disease.

Ed is not the only person to be confused about AIDS. Because AIDS first appeared in the early 1980s, doctors and researchers have not had much time to study it. They don't yet know everything about the disease. But they are learning more every day.

AIDS stands for acquired immune deficiency syndrome. Each of us has an *immune system*. It helps us fight off germs that make us sick and helps us get better when we do get sick. A person with AIDS has a weakened immune system.

AIDS is caused by a virus called *HIV.* That stands for *human immunodeficiency virus*. HIV lives in an infected person's bodily fluids. The four body fluids that are known to transmit HIV are blood, a man's semen, a woman's vaginal fluids and breast milk. Sweat, tears, and saliva are also body fluids, but researchers have found that there is not enough HIV in these fluids to infect another person.

When the immune system is weakened by HIV, it is easier for a person to get sick. That's because the immune system is too weak to fight off germs and infection. If a person with AIDS becomes sick, it is harder for him or her to get well.

For example, Henry and Sam are best friends. Sam has AIDS. One day they ate lunch at a table where someone had sneezed earlier. Both Henry and Sam were exposed to the flu virus, but Henry's immune system fought the virus. He did not get sick. Sam's immune system was too weak to fight the virus. Sam not only

AIDS is caused by a virus called HIV. This virus lives in body fluids such as tears, saliva, blood and urine.

got sick, he had to stay in a hospital. His weakened immune system could not help him get better.

AIDS is an STD because it can be spread sexually. Intimate contact with an infected man's semen or an infected woman's vaginal fluids are two ways to get AIDS.

When people are infected with HIV, they usually do not get sick right away. In fact, they may carry the virus for many years before they develop symptoms. But even though they may not have symptoms, they can still spread the virus to other people.

People with AIDS may develop many symptoms when they first become sick. These include fevers, diarrhea, night sweats, exhaustion and swollen glands. But these are also symptoms of other diseases. The only way to tell for sure if a person has AIDS is by going to a doctor and having the blood tested for HIV.

Some people with AIDS develop a cancer called *Kaposi's sarcoma*. This appears as dark, often purplish patches on the skin. A person with AIDS can also develop pneumonia or other severe infections. Although there are many exceptions, people with full-blown AIDS usually die two to three years after their first symptoms appear.

At first, most of the people with AIDS in the United States were *homosexual* men. A homosexual, or *gay*, man is a man who is sexually attracted to other men. People who are attracted to members of the opposite sex are called *heterosexual*, or *straight*. For a long time,

Condoms and other forms of birth control are available at drugstores.

many straight people thought that they couldn't get AIDS. This is not true. Today, straight people have been developing AIDS at a faster rate than any other group. While homosexuals still make up a large percentage of people with AIDS, the gay community has done a lot about teaching people about safer sex. And the number of gay men becoming infected with HIV has dropped dramatically.

There is no cure for AIDS. Scientists have developed two drugs, however, that seem to help people with AIDS live longer. These drugs are *AZT* and *DDI*. They are also given to people who test positive for HIV but don't have any symptoms of AIDS. Both drugs slow down the spread of HIV in a person's cells.

As with other STDs, the best way to avoid getting AIDS is to practice safer sex.

OTHER STDs

Vaginitis is an infection common among women. It most often occurs in sexually active women. Men who have had intercourse with a woman with vaginitis can develop symptoms as well.

The two most common types of vaginitis are called *candidiasis* and *trichomonias*. They are caused by different germs, but the symptoms are similar: discharges from the vagina or penis, an itching and burning sensation in the genitals, and pain during intercourse.

A doctor can recommend a variety of drugs to cure vaginitis. Anyone who is treated, however, should make sure that his or her sex partner is also examined and treated. Otherwise there is a good chance that the partners will continue to reinfect each other.

Chlamydia infections are similar to vaginitis infections, but they infect the urinary passage. This passage is called the *urethra*. *Chlamydia* is a type of bacteria that causes a common sexually transmitted infection called *nonspecific urethritis (NSU)*. Symptoms include pain and burning during urination, and a watery, milky discharge from the penis or vagina. As with vaginitis, both sex partners should be treated by a doctor at the same time.

If untreated, chlamydia can lead to *pelvic inflammatory disease (PID)*. PID is an infection that can cause permanent damage to a woman's reproductive system.

Genital warts can infect any region of the genital or anal area. Like other types of warts, they are caused by a virus. Genital warts are one of the most common STDs. They can be spread from partner to partner by direct or indirect contact. They also can be spread from one area of a person's body to another area. If left untreated, these warts may become very large. Doctors now believe that untreated warts can lead to cancer.

Since the warts are painless, a woman may not find out if she is infected unless she is examined by a doctor.

Genital warts can be removed during minor surgery or can be treated with chemicals. However, sometimes new warts appear as the old ones are destroyed. Also, warts very often reappear after treatment. To limit the spread of these warts, an infected person should seek treatment when the warts are still small.

Scabies and lice are very contagious STDs caused by parasitic bugs. Scabies and lice are not infections; they are *infestations*. They are usually spread from person to person by close physical contact. They can also be spread by sharing infested clothing, towels or sheets.

The scabies bug actually lives beneath the surface of the skin. Four to six weeks after coming in contact with scabies, the infested person will develop a rash. This rash is extremely itchy. The rash looks like tiny blisters, bumps or white streaks.

Lice live on an infested person's skin. They bite through the skin and suck blood for food. Lice (also known as *crabs*) are common STDs, much more common than scabies. Lice leave tiny eggs on the hair of the infested area. These eggs hatch in about seven days. Like scabies, lice are extremely itchy. Unlike scabies, lice are large enough to be seen by the human eye.

A doctor can prescribe or recommend lotions that will kill these parasites. Clothing, towels and sheets should be washed so that the scabies or lice on them will also be killed.

MAYBE IT WILL GO AWAY

Kris tossed and turned in her bed all night. Eventually she woke up, but she was still exhausted. She noticed that her sheets were very wet. She had been sweating a lot.

Kris touched her neck. Her throat was still swollen. It had been that way all week. Exhaustion, night sweats, swollen glands . . . she knew these all could be symptoms of AIDS.

"It can't be," she whispered to herself. "I can't have it."

She thought back to two years ago. She had been in love with a man named Barry, who had had a drug problem. He'd always promised to quit, but he'd never stopped. In fact, he had started taking harder drugs, even heroin.

Kris had broken up with Barry a few weeks after she'd first noticed needle marks on his arm. She had tried to help him, but he'd seemed determined to take drugs.

Recently Kris had heard that Barry had died. She'd

Teens are often frightened or embarrassed about STDs. But it is very important to seek medical attention as soon as symptoms appear.

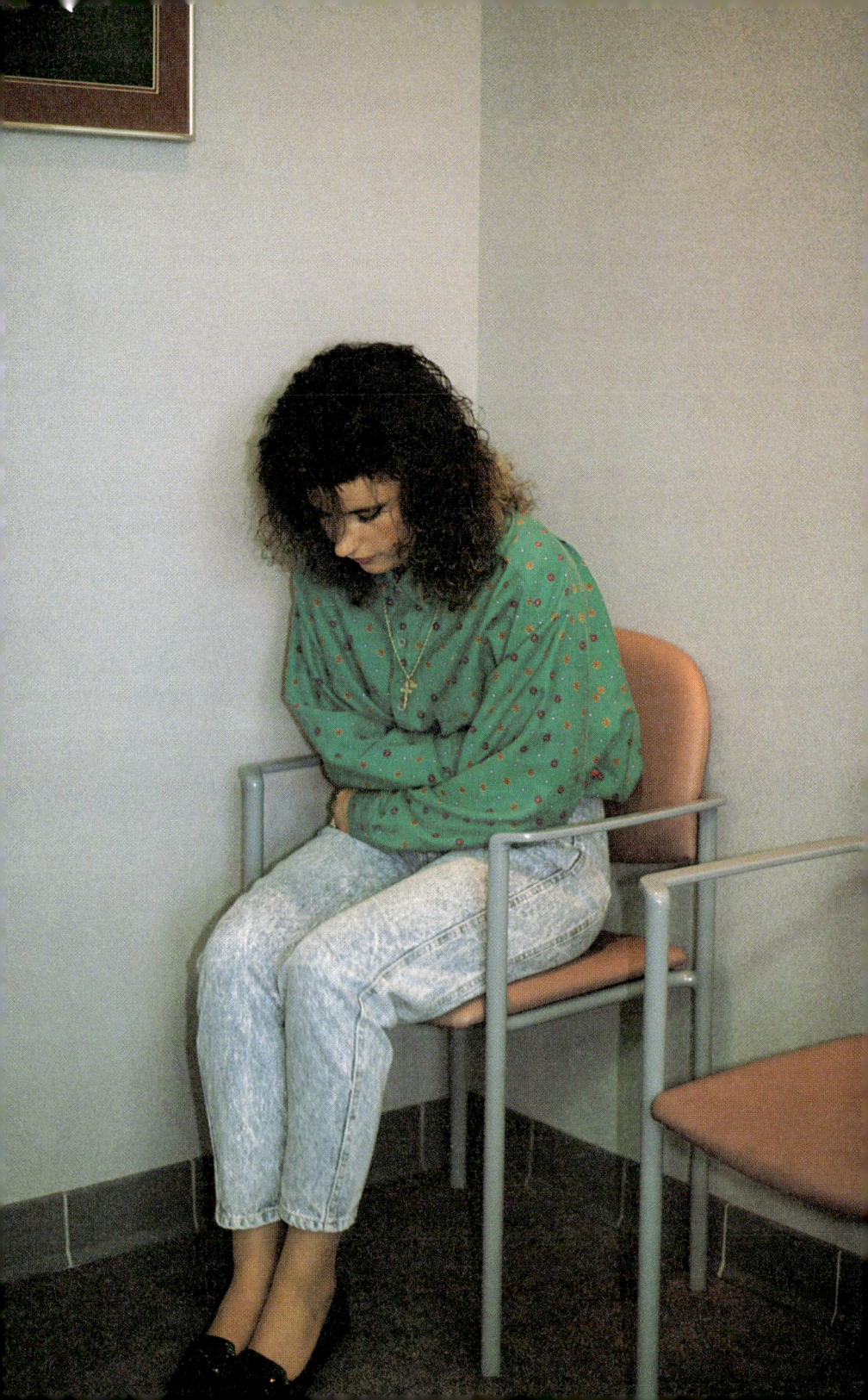

assumed that he had overdosed on heroin or some other kind of drug. But she knew that many drug addicts who shared needles were now dying of AIDS. Could it be that Barry also had died of AIDS?

Kris tried to push this thought from her mind. She refused to consider the idea that Barry might have given her the virus that causes AIDS. Maybe the symptoms she had would just go away. And if they didn't, then she'd deal with them later.

This kind of denial is common among people who think they might have an STD. They often are too frightened or too embarrassed to take the next step and go to a doctor.

But it is crucial to seek medical treatment as soon as a symptom is recognized. In Kris's case, she didn't seek treatment until she became very sick with pneumonia and was hospitalized. If she had gone to her doctor as soon as she recognized her symptoms, the doctor might have prescribed AZT or another drug that could have kept her from getting so sick. These medicines are more effective when the patient is healthier.

With most STDs, the longer a person waits to be treated, the longer it will take to get healthy again. An infected person also runs the risk of having the disease spread to other parts of the body and do serious damage. And, of course, as long as a person is infected, he or she can pass the STD on to other people.

STDs don't just go away. Sooner or later, they have to be dealt with. And sooner is definitely better than later.

WHAT SHOULD I DO?

Mary was sure she had an STD. But she didn't seek treatment right away because she didn't know who to turn to. She was afraid to ask her parents for help—they might be angry with her. She was embarrassed to confide in her friends—they might laugh at her.

She finally got up the nerve to tell her sister, Jen. Mary was amazed at how relieved she felt to share her problem. And her sister didn't lecture her or laugh. Jen gave her the name of her doctor. She even volunteered to escort Mary for moral support.

Suddenly Mary felt a lot better. With the help of Jen, she would get through this experience. She realized that family members and friends are there to help you. They don't want to see you sick.

There are other options for people who think they might have an STD. Most cities and large towns have public health agencies and Planned Parenthood clinics. The agencies can offer affordable suggestions. The Planned Parenthood clinics usually treat STDs as well. Their addresses and phone numbers are listed in the phone book.

Several toll-free hotlines are available to answer questions. The counselors on these hotlines provide information and can recommend a doctor or clinic in your area. Some of these phone numbers are listed in the back of this book.

← **EMERGENCY / TRAUMA CENTER**
← Clinic
← Receiving Dept.
← Dean St. - South
Engle St. - North →

Common Sexually Transmitted Diseases

- AIDS - CHLAMYDIA
- GONORRHEA - *syphilis*
- TRICHOMONAS VAGINALIS
- HERPES SIMPLEX - NGU
- crabs - ...

DISEASE	FIRST SYMPTOMS USUALLY APPEAR	USUAL SYMPTOMS	TRANSMISSION	
AIDS Acquired Immune Deficiency Syndrome Cause: HIV virus	Several months to several years	Night sweats. Swollen glands. Unexplained weight loss. Persistent cough. Fatigue. Chronic diarrhea. Persistent blue and brown skin lesions and oral thrush (white spots in mouth)	Repeated sexual intercourse with partner or partners having infected body fluids. Sharing of contaminated needles.	
GONORRHEA (called clap, drip, drip) Cause: bacteria	2 - 10 days (up to 30 days)	White or yellow discharge from genitals or anus. Pain on urination or defecation. Pharyngeal infections are usually without symptoms. Women: Low abdominal pain especially after period. May have no symptoms. Men: May have no symptoms.	Direct contact of infected mucous membrane with the urethra, cervix, anus, throat or eyes.	
SYPHILIS (called syph, pox, bad blood) Cause: spirochete	10 - 90 days (usually 3 weeks)	1st STAGE: Chancre (painless pimple, blister or sore) where germs entered body, i.e. genitals, anus, lips, breast, etc. 2nd STAGE: Rash or mucous patches (most are highly infectious), spotty hair loss, sore throat, swollen glands. Symptoms may recur for up to 2 years.	Direct contact with infectious sore, rashes or mucous patches.	
HERPES SIMPLEX (called herpes) Cause: virus	Highly variable	Cluster of tender, painful blisters. Painful urination. Swollen glands and fever. Feeling of malaise.	Direct contact with blisters or open sores.	
VAGINITIS TRICHOMONAS VAGINALIS	Varies with causative organism (1-4 weeks)	Heavy, frothy discharge. Intense itching, burning and redness.	Direct contact with infected area.	
CANDIDA (yeast infection)		Thick, cheesy discharge. Intense itching and skin irritation.		
VAGINOSIS GARDNERELLA		Vaginal discharge with fishy odor.		
NON-GONOCOCCAL URETHRITIS CHLAMYDIA UREA PLASMA	7 - 14 days	Watery, white discharge. Discomfort while urinating. Woman may have bleeding (non-menstrual).	Direct contact with infected area.	
VENEREAL WARTS (called genital warts condylomata acuminata) Cause: virus	1 - 3 months	Local irritation, itching and wart-like growths usually on the genitals, anus or throat.	Direct contact with warts.	
MOLLUSCUM CONTAGIOSUM Cause: virus		Small, round, shiny flesh-colored papules.		
ECTO-PARASITES PEDICULOSIS PUBIS (called crabs, cooties) Cause: 6-legged louse SCABIES (called itch mite)	4 - 3 weeks	Intense itching, pinhead blood spots on underwear, nits in hair. Intense itching at night, raised gray lines on skin.	Direct contact with infected area or clothes and bedding which contain lice or nits. Direct contact with infected area or clothes and bedding containing mites.	

There may be someone at your church or school who can help. A clergyman, teacher, school nurse or guidance counselor may be able to steer you in the right direction. And they will keep your problem confidential.

TREATMENTS AND CURES

As you now know, there is a wide variety of sexually transmitted diseases. Each disease has its own unique set of symptoms. Likewise, each disease has its own treatment or cure.

Most STDs can be treated only by a doctor. When you tell your doctor your symptoms, he or she will probably run some tests on you. Your doctor may ask for a urine sample or take a blood test. Any kind of sore you may have will be examined. Your doctor will use a microscope to look at anything unusual, such as a discharge from your genitals.

In some cases, a doctor will not have to take any tests. After examining you, he or she may be able to tell what kind of disease you have.

In other cases, you will have to wait about a week for the results of your tests to come back. Once the doctor has reviewed your tests, a treatment or cure can be prescribed.

At one time, syphilis and gonorrhea had no cure. Now these diseases can be cured by shots of penicillin

Most cities and large towns have public health clinics that can treat people with STDs.

or some other kind of antibiotic. The longer you wait to be treated, the more shots you will have to have.

Herpes and AIDS still have no cure. But researchers have developed some drugs to ease the pain and prevent recurrences of illness. Because cures for syphilis and gonorrhea were found, there is great hope that one day there will be cures for herpes and AIDS. Doctors are working hard to understand these diseases better and to find cures for them.

The other STDs can be treated with chemicals, lotions or drugs. Your doctor will recommend the best treatment for you.

TELLING PARTNERS

"But, Dr. Broder, I promised," Jason pleaded. "I swore to her that I wouldn't tell anyone about that night."

Jason rubbed his eyes wearily. It had been a long, upsetting day. First he'd found out that he had gonorrhea. Now his doctor wanted Rita's name and phone number.

He looked at Dr. Broder again. "Maybe she's not infected. If she was, she'd take care of it herself."

"Not necessarily, Jason. Women can't always see the symptoms of gonorrhea. That's why it's important that she is examined by a doctor as soon as possible."

Jason felt very guilty. Rita hadn't wanted to have sex until they were married. But he had threatened to break up with her if they didn't develop a sexual relationship.

Then, after making love for the first time, Jason had broken up with Rita anyway. She just didn't seem to be as exciting as some of the other girls he had been with recently.

Rita had been crushed, and Jason had felt like a monster. Now it seemed cruel to tell her that she might have gonorrhea. Hadn't he caused her enough unhappiness?

Couples who are sexually active need to be honest with each other when it comes to issues like STDs.

And what about her parents? They were friends with his parents. Would they all find out? Jason didn't want his mother or father to know about this, and he was sure that Rita would feel the same way.

Dr. Broder's voice interrupted Jason's thoughts. "I know what you must be going through. But would you be able to stand knowing that this woman might infect other men? Or that she might never be able to have a baby?"

"No," Jason said in a weak voice. "I know you're right. I guess it's time to take responsibility for my actions."

One of the most difficult things about having an STD is telling partners. But an infected person must let his or her partners know for several reasons.

First of all, the partners may not realize that they've been exposed to a disease. They may have no symptoms, or they might not recognize the symptoms. If untreated, there is a risk that the disease will spread to other parts of the body and do serious damage.

Second, a person who has just been cured might once again have sexual relations with a former partner. If this partner is still infected, the cured person might be infected with the disease again. This won't happen if the partner is told and cured.

Finally, infected partners need to know so they will not spread the STDs to new partners. The only way to bring these epidemic diseases under control is to treat all known cases.

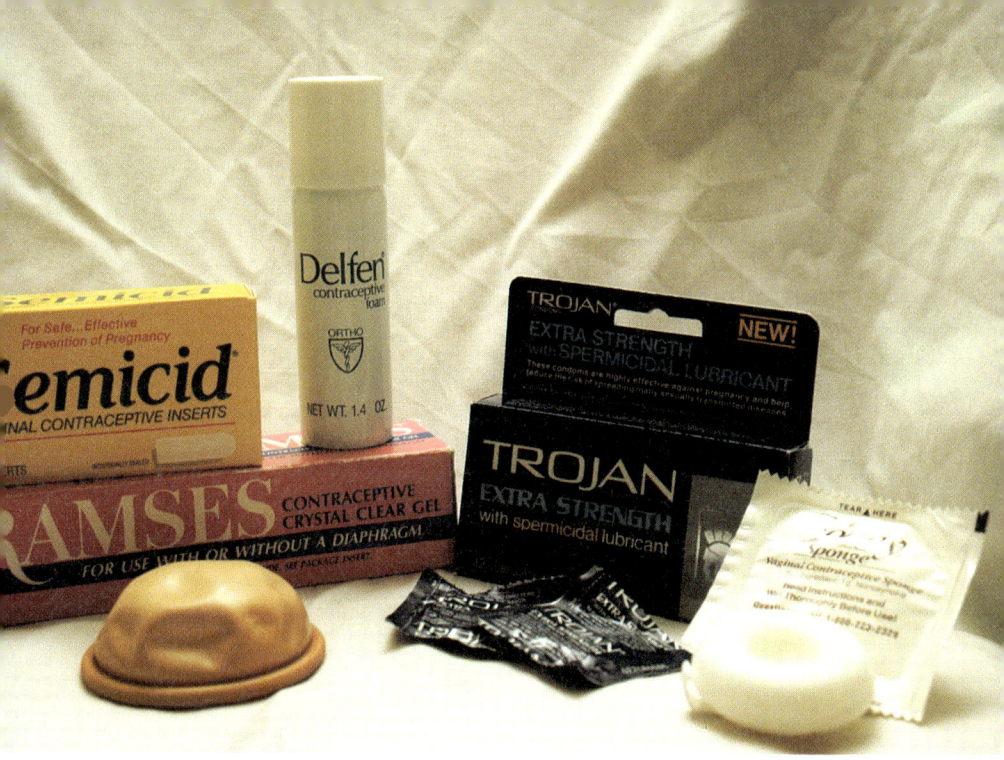

Many different kinds of birth control are available today. Condoms are most effective at preventing transmission of STDs.

NEXT TIME: PREVENTION

Annette has been dating Will for six months. Many of her friends have had sex with their boyfriends, but Annette has decided to wait. She wants to be sure that her relationship with Will is going to be a permanent one.

41

This is called *abstinence*. Abstinence is the only sure way to avoid getting an STD (or getting pregnant). With all the talk about STDs and unwanted pregnancy, many people have decided to abstain from sex until they are ready for a permanent relationship.

Barbara is one of Annette's friends. She is sexually active with her boyfriend, but she takes certain precautions to avoid getting an STD.

First, Barbara has only one sex partner—her boyfriend. She and her boyfriend don't make love with anyone but each other. They know that the more sex partners a person has, the greater the chance of getting a venereal disease.

Second, Barbara and her boyfriend always use condoms. They are made of latex and fit closely over the penis. Condoms help keep a man's genitals and semen from coming into direct contact with his partners genitals and bodily fluids. Wearing condoms cannot always prevent the spread of some diseases, such as herpes, lice and genital warts. But condoms do reduce the risk of spreading syphilis, gonorrhea and HIV.

Third, Barbara goes to her *gynecologist* for regular checkups. A gynecologist is a doctor who specializes in women's health. Barbara knows that some STDs, such as vaginitis, are more common among sexually active women. Her doctor gives her regular tests and examinations for STDs.

FEELING GOOD ABOUT YOURSELF

Joey smiles as he walks by the health center. It has been a year since he was treated there for his STD. He has learned a lot from that unpleasant experience.

He now limits his sex partners and uses condoms. He knows that one unsafe time is all it takes to get an STD.

He knows that there are many people who can help when he might be in trouble—family, friends, teachers,

Sexually active people of all ages and ethnic backgrounds are vulnerable to STDs. That's why everyone needs to get the facts and act smart.

doctors, members of the clergy. These people can provide information, understanding and support.

He knows that he should see a doctor immediately if another symptom ever appears. Waiting only makes the problem worse.

He knows that STDs can happen to anyone—old or young, rich or poor, smart or ignorant. People with STDs are not bad or dirty. Rather, they are not well and need medical attention.

Everyone can learn from Joey's experiences. To feel good about ourselves, we have to take responsibility for our actions.

FOR MORE INFORMATION

AIDS National Hotline
(800) 342-AIDS

American Social Health Association
260 Sheridan Avenue
Palo Alto, CA 94306
(415) 327-6465

VD National Hotline
(800) 227-8922
In California: (800) 982-5883

GLOSSARY/INDEX

ABSTINENCE 42—*The choice not to be sexually active.*
AIDS (ACQUIRED IMMUNO DEFICIENCY SYNDROME) 8, 9, 21–23, 25–26, 28, 32, 33, 38, 40—*A sexually transmitted disease of the immune system, which almost always leads to death.*
ANTIBIOTICS 12, 17, 38—*Medicine that can kill bacteria.*
AZT 28, 34—*A medicine that helps fight HIV.*
BACTERIA 8, 9, 17, 29—*Tiny plants that live in animals, plants, soil and water.*
CANDIDIASIS 28—*A common type of vaginitis.*
CHANCRE 17—*The first symptom of syphilis; it is a hard, painless, red sore.*
CHLAMYDIA 29—*A type of bacteria that causes urethral infections.*
CONDOM 5, 11, 19, 20, 42, 43—*A latex sheath worn over the penis to protect against disease and/or pregnancy.*
CRABS 31—*Another name for lice.*
DDI 28—*A medicine that helps fight HIV.*
GAY 26—*Another term for homosexual.*
GENITAL WARTS 8, 29, 40—*An infection of the genitals caused by a virus.*
GONORRHEA 8, 9, 10–12, 29, 37, 38, 40—*A sexu-*

ally transmitted disease caused by bacteria.
GYNECOLOGIST 42—*A doctor who specializes in women's health.*
HERPES 8, 9, 18–21, 38, 40—*Sexually transmitted virus that causes sores on the mouth or genital areas.*
HETEROSEXUAL 28—*A person attracted to members of the opposite sex.*
HIV (HUMAN IMMUNODEFICIENCY VIRUS) 25, 26, 28, 42—*The virus associated with AIDS.*
HOMOSEXUAL 26—*A person who is sexually attracted to others of the same sex.*
HOST 9—*A person or animal on which a parasite lives.*
IMMUNE SYSTEM 25—*The body's internal system that fights off illness.*
INFEST 31—*To overrun or occur in large numbers so as to be troublesome or harmful.*
KAPOSI'S SARCOMA 26—*A skin cancer common in people with AIDS.*
LATENT SYPHILIS 17—*The third and final stage of syphilis.*
LICE 8, 9, 31–32, 40—*Tiny parasites that live on a host's skin.*
NONSPECIFIC URETHRITIS (NSU) 29—*Infection of the urethra.*
PARASITE 8, 9, 31–32—*A bug or animal that lives on the blood of another living organism.*
PELVIC INFLAMMATORY DISEASE (PID) 29—*An infection that can cause permanent damage to a woman's reproductive system.*

PENICILLIN 12, 17, 21, 37—*The most widely prescribed antibiotic.*
RECURRENCE 20, 38—*The return of an illness after a period of time.*
SAFER SEX 11, 15, 19, 28—*The practice of using condoms during sexual activity in order to prevent the spread of sexually transmitted diseases.*
SCABIES 8, 9, 31–32—*Parasites that live under a host's skin.*
SECONDARY SYPHILIS 17—*The second stage of the syphilis disease, characterized by a rash, fever, headaches, loss of appetite and weariness.*
SEXUALLY TRANSMITTED DISEASE 5, 8–9, 11, 14, 15, 16, 26, 29, 31, 32, 34, 35, 37, 38, 40, 42, 43, 44—*A disease that is usually spread during intimate sexual contact.*
STRAIGHT 28—*Another term for heterosexual.*
SYMPTOM 5, 12, 14, 16–17, 26, 28, 29, 32, 34, 37, 40, 44—*A sign of a physical illness.*
SYPHILIS 8, 9, 14, 17, 37, 38, 40—*An STD caused by bacteria.*
TRICHOMONIASIS 28—*A common type of vaginitis.*
URETHRA 29—*The passage through which urine travels.*
VAGINITIS 28–29, 42—*An inflammation or infection of the vagina.*
VENEREAL DISEASE (VD) 5, 8, 42—*A sexually transmitted disease.*
VIRUS 8, 9, 20, 25–26, 28, 29—*A tiny germ that causes illness.*